a gorgeous sense of hope

a love fable

emma magenta

**Andrews McMeel
Publishing, LLC**

Kansas City

For information, write Andrews McMeel Publishing, LLC, an Andrews McMeel Universal
company, 4520 Main Street, Kansas City, Missouri 64111.

07 08 09 10 SDB 10 9 8 7 6 5 4 3 2
ISBN-13: 978-0-7407-6068-6
ISBN-10: 0-7407-6068-8
Library of Congress Control Number: 2006922722

ATTENTION: SCHOOLS AND BUSINESSES
Andrews McMeel books are available at quantity discounts with bulk purchase
for educational, business, or sales promotional use. For information, please write to:
Special Sales Department, Andrews McMeel Publishing, LLC, 4520 Main Street,
Kansas City, Missouri 64111.

dedicated to Arturo Aguirre.

thank you for being a beacon
of light after an era of woe.

acknowledgments

much love and thanks to Bradley Trevor Grieve, for opening the door with a generous heart.

thank you to Chris Schillig from Andrews McMeel, for being such an inspired, patient, and generous editor.

a gorgeous thanx to Jane Palfreyman from Random House Australia for your great support, advice, and humor.

Al Zuckerman from Writers House: thank you for your advice and for nurturing my naive little self to greater understanding.

Simon Bekker, dear friend and gorgeous mover of the elements to greater beauty: thank you for designing my second offspring.

thanx also to Lane Butler, Maya Rock, and Anita Arnold, for your assistance at various intervals as well.

Other warmth givers: My magnificent family, Arturo, Louwe, Rox, Rakkers, Liza, Mags, Sog, Abi, Detty,

Ginny, Sophie Pigeon, Ariana, Shaun, Pedro, Andy, Ross, and Maxine (all Berkelouw Books love children), Becky, and of course Indiana Queenie.

finally, thanks to my posse of gorgeous darlings at www.capoeira.com.au (muito axé!).

She became a cartographer of the heart.

there was once a girl who had secured
for herself a relationship of
considerable consequence.

this was a feat not entirely amazing in itself.

but for one who had known nothing more
than a soufflé of promises,

Sssshhh!

a cosmic joke in want of a punch line.

the achievement was, to say the least,

remarkable!

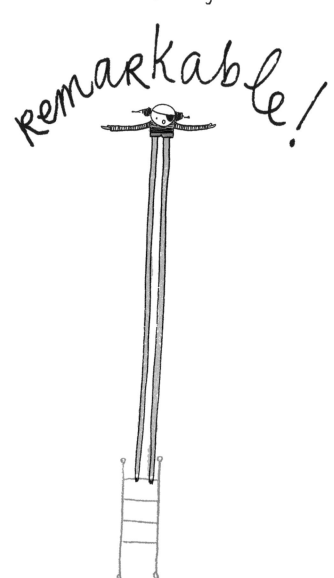

in the shadow of such dismal encounters thus far,
the authenticity of this love was illuminated
like a rare constellation.

it was a magical union
built on a gorgeous intimacy,

a shared love of extreme sports,

and comedy as a way of life.

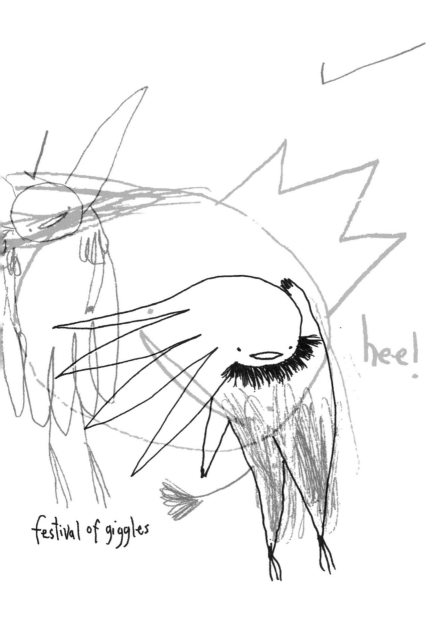

hee!

festival of giggles

her friends, somewhat dubious,
waited offstage ready for action.

they recalled only too
well how she looked

the last time she felt this in love.

a sprained heart

rather than lament her wasted youth
spent nurturing fools,

She abandoned her history
with a simple word

and embarked on this new love expedition
with only eternal optimism as a compass.

the Summer Months

swashbuckling boots for courage

hoping to navigate this relationship
with greater foresight, she looked around for
a positive sign that she was indeed
heading in the right direction.

encouraged by the recurrence
of the number 2 in her life
(an omen that their relationship
was indeed auspicious),

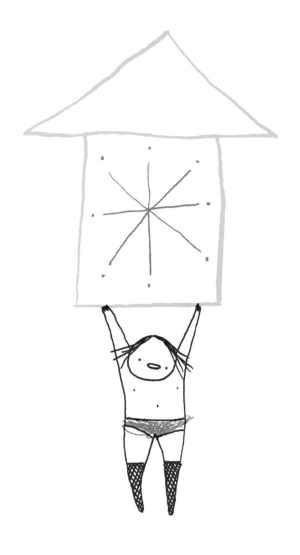

she consolidated their love
with four walls,

...ikebana

zen furnishings,

a gosling

and substitute offspring.

this arrangement enveloped their love
like an exquisite bubble

and aided her conviction that this was
clearly the peak of her love career to date.

as a result, she felt a new
freedom of acceptance to finally
come out as an elk in his presence.

stand arms akimbo,

shake the antlers,
(like this)

"dance of the elk"

then, be very still.

the Autumn Months

she watched herself wilt.

having found their bearings, the ease
of each other's company was a relief.

her friends observed her joy and warmed
to the notion that he was not just another jester.

but it wasn't long before cracks
in the structure were apparent to her.

what seemed like calm waters
quickly became the Bermuda Triangle,

as the blessed pair
sailed into the
insidious zone of complacency.

acts of devotion were forfeited
when unexpectedly,

like the sobering effects of daylight
on a nightclub dance floor,

their more hidden selves took
center stage for an indefinite period.

curiosity about each other's world
hit a terrific speed bump

as they watched the magnificent wave
of passion that once existed between them

dwindle to a ripple.

and eventually, a drought.

exquisite speech patterns that had once
made up their dialogue were now broken,

replaced with a canyon of silence.

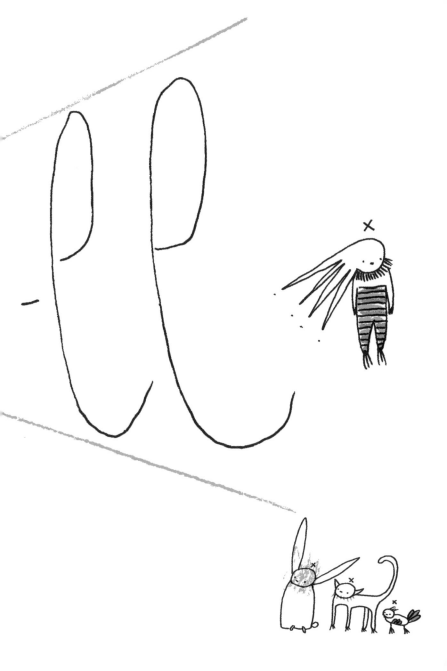

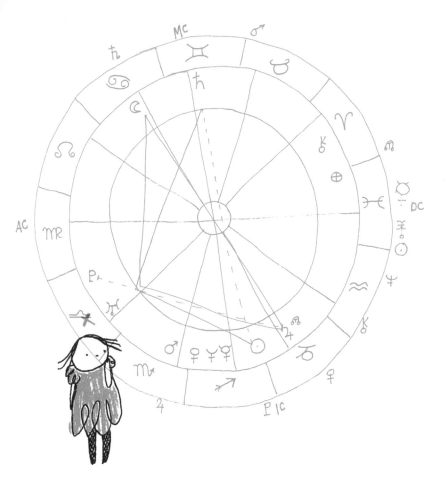

anxious for a reprieve,
she consulted heavenly charts
to pinpoint upcoming joy,

but the gold moments of bliss
became so infrequent that when they
did arise, she considered cloning
herself to maintain the experience.

maybe new earrings will help.

Soon they both looked outside for solutions

"just friends"

and reassurance that the passion that defined them would not expire in a kitchen filled with white goods.

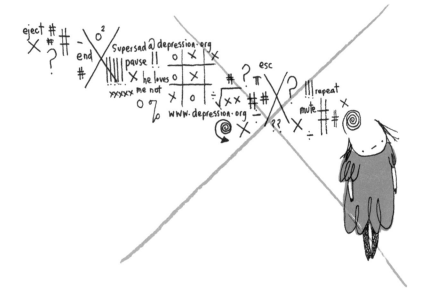

the strong aromatic scent of well-known
terrain wafted by her, as she pondered
whether again she had toiled for naught
in the realm of the heart.

the Winter Months

she hid herself in hair

rejecting the notion that she had sailed
on yet another emotional shipwreck,

she searched her surrounds
for an omen synonymous with luck,

like a charm of gold finches

or the foot of a rabbit.

in the absence of such encouraging aid,

she waved him a temporary "au revoir"
and set off into the unknown
in search of a solution.

she cocooned.

tying a cord to her wrist,
she anchored herself to the part inside
that houses infinite love,

where she beseeched her
favorite selves for expert navigation.

in this cocoon it occurred to her
that her choices were simple.

She could let this love be blown
about by the whim of happenstance,

excessive
jealousy
creative inertia
fear
paranoia
boredom.

exposed to the elements that
would one day foster its decay.

or she could take action
to liberate them both
from this emotional quagmire.

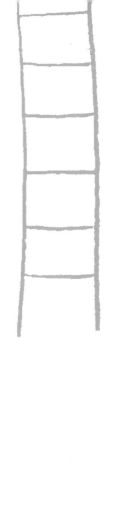

her internal map suggested
that she steer this once-promising
relationship to its zenith

and seek the highest possible
version of their union every day.

love as alchemy,

love as art.

the Spring Months

she put in fresh thoughts.

With renewed hope, she adorned
fresh feet for a new direction,

and having a quick word
with Sir Edmund Hillary,

She made her way back to where
her greatest love had retreated.

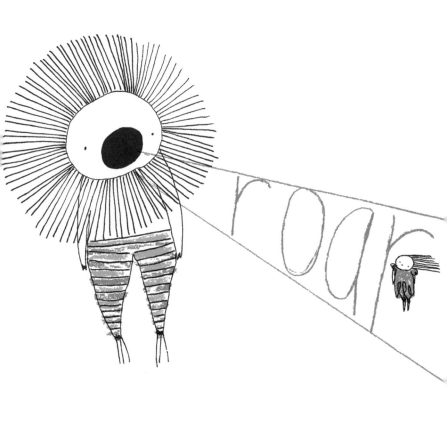

in response to her emotional absence,
his countenance was somewhat humorless

undeterred, she just put on her
favorite dress for confidence and
played a little tune until he warmed.

a mild amnesty was achieved by this act of peaceful protest,

So she sent him a Morse code message to see if he was contactable for conversation.

much to her delight, she spied
some hope through the dark
when he threw back a reply.

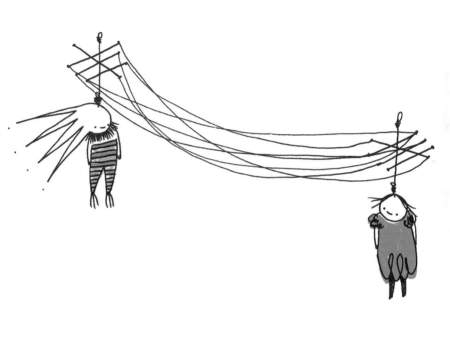

tuning into each other again,
she plugged them into unknown frequencies
of worlds yet to be discovered

and created a structure of
interdependence built on gorgeous
new floorboards of trust.

gorgeous

big

feelings.

a love concert was arranged,
accessible only via canoe,

she leaked passion.

and before long, it was clear
she had invented something different
and very exciting between them.